Nina KWOW

by Natalie Behar
illustrated by Nicole Tadgell

Harcourt
SCHOOL PUBLISHERS

Printed in China

ISBN 10: 0-15-350559-1
ISBN 13: 978-0-15-350559-1

Ordering Options
ISBN 10: 0-15-350335-1 (Grade 5 Below-Level Collection)
ISBN 13: 978-0-15-350335-1 (Grade 5 Below-Level Collection)
ISBN 10: 0-15-357560-3 (package of 5)
ISBN 13: 978-0-15-357560-0 (package of 5)

4 5 6 7 8 9 10   0940   12 11 10 09

CAST

NINA	SEAN
GRAN	JAKE
ALEX	TORY
BLAIR SKYLAR	RECEPTIONIST
MR. FINKS	CAMERAPERSON

Act One

NINA *sits on the edge of the stage with a notebook in her lap and a pencil in her hand. Her grandmother, GRAN, watches television in a nearby "room," where her brother, ALEX, polishes a pair of shoes. NINA sighs loudly. She stands up and walks into the living area.*

NINA: Gran?

GRAN: Yes, honey?

NINA: Tomorrow I have to give a presentation to my class. I have to tell them what I want to be when I grow up. I'm stuck. Will you help me?

ALEX: A little kid like you is never going to grow up!

GRAN: Oh, hush, Alex! We'll figure something out, Nina.

GRAN *turns down the TV.* NINA *sits.*

GRAN: Now what are you thinking?

NINA: I know I like to do research, and I'm interested in speech and communication. I want to do something that relates to . . . well, *everything.*

GRAN: *(Laughs)* That is a tough place to start. Don't worry. I'm sure you will think of something, sweetie.

The news comes on the TV. ALEX *turns the volume back up.*

BLAIR SKYLAR: *(Offstage)* Now, in the latest KWOW news, the local government is trying to decide whether . . .

GRAN: Alex, I think you've monopolized the television enough tonight. I'd like to watch my programs now.

GRAN *reaches toward the remote control.*

NINA: *(Enraptured by the screen)* Wait! Gran, what if I could be a TV reporter—like Blair Skylar?

GRAN: I don't see why you couldn't.

NINA *picks up her notebook and runs out of the room.*

NINA: You were a great help, Gran! Thanks.

GRAN: *(Laughs to herself)* My pleasure.

Act Two, Scene 1

The stage is set like a classroom: students sit in rows of desks, and their teacher, MR. FINKS, *sits at his desk.* SEAN *stands in front of the class.*

SEAN: . . . and that's why, when I grow up, I'm going to be a dentist who fixes people's teeth without pain. *The students applaud loudly.*

MR. FINKS: That is very enterprising of you. I'm glad you've decided to become a dentist. I think you will make an excellent dentist.

SEAN *takes his seat.*

MR. FINKS: Nina, you're next.

NINA: *(Stands up in the front)* Hi. I'm Nina Pua, but you know that already. *(Laughter)* I'm just practicing saying my name for my newfound profession. You see, I've decided to become a television news reporter. I'm not going to wait until I grow up—because who knows if that will ever happen. *(More laughter)* I've decided to start now. If you want the latest news, tune in to KWOW news, and you can learn what's going on—from me!

NINA *takes her seat. The students look at her, confused.*

JAKE: How are you going to do that?

NINA: I'm going there after school to apply for a job.

TORY: You're only twelve. Don't you have to be at least fifteen to have a job?

NINA: *(Stammers)* Well, I . . . then I'll work for free!

MR. FINKS: Regardless, Jake, it's your turn.

JAKE *slowly shuffles to the front of the class.*

JAKE: When I grow up, I'm going to be the world's greatest . . .

Act Two, Scene 2

NINA *walks into the* KWOW *reception area.*

RECEPTIONIST: May I help you?

NINA: I'm here to apply for a job.

RECEPTIONIST: How old are you, dear? Do you have an appointment?

BLAIR SKYLAR *and a* CAMERAPERSON *walk in.*

BLAIR SKYLAR: Any messages, Jackie?

RECEPTIONIST: No. This girl is here about a job.

NINA: Hi, I'm Nina Pua, and I want to be a television reporter—

BLAIR SKYLAR: Isn't she cute? Sadly, I'm afraid this job isn't for children. *(To the CAMERAPERSON)* We better head out.

RECEPTIONIST: Why don't you come back in about fifteen years?

Act Three

NINA *sits on a bench, completely deflated.* JAKE, TORY, *and* SEAN *approach, bouncing a basketball.*

TORY: What's wrong, Nina?

JAKE: Didn't get that job, eh?

TORY *motions to him to be quiet.*

NINA: *(Somberly)* I'm too young, like everyone thought.

They sit down next to her and bounce the ball back and forth between them.

SEAN: I hate it when people assume you can't do things just because you're young.

NINA: I know what you mean.

TORY: What if we found a way to *show* them that you could do it? Like what if—

SEAN: We made our own news!

JAKE: We'll ask to use my dad's video camera!

The three students run offstage. When they return, JAKE is holding his father's video camera.

SEAN: Jake, that was incredibly nice of your father to let us borrow his camera.

NINA: Yes, now all we need is a story.

They pause, trying to think of a good story.

TORY: *(Sniffs and looks into the distance)* What's that?

SEAN: The sky?

JAKE: Don't you see smoke?

NINA: Oh, no! It looks like the school is on fire! Let's get over there! *(They run to the other side of the stage.)* Jake, the camera!

JAKE *fumbles with the camera.*

TORY: Okay, let's go!

As NINA *begins speaking,* BLAIR SKYLAR *and the* CAMERAPERSON *appear on the scene and begin setting up. They seem to be having some technical difficulties with their equipment.* NINA *has begun her report.*

NINA: This is Nina Pua reporting live from our school that appears to be on fire! Billows of smoke are appearing near the science wing. *(Sirens are heard in the distance.)* More firefighters are on their way. Thankfully, this has occurred after school adjourned for the day. Otherwise, evacuating students and teachers from the entire school would be a cumbersome affair. But look—the smoke has already started to clear.

BLAIR SKYLAR: Have we missed it?

CAMERAPERSON: Oh, no! Not again . . .

JAKE: We've got the whole thing on video.

BLAIR SKYLAR: Really? Can we use it?

The kids look at NINA.

NINA: Are we going to get credit?

BLAIR SKYLAR: Of course! *(Looks apologetically at* NINA*)* Are you the girl I saw at the TV station? Wow, I really misjudged you. I thought because you were a kid, you couldn't do this job. I was really wrong.

CAMERAPERSON: You kids sure seem to know what you're doing.

SEAN: Do you think there's any chance school will be cancelled tomorrow?

JAKE: If it is, it'll make the news!

NINA: Not before we do!

BLAIR SKYLAR: If school is cancelled, you should come down to the station. I'm going to recommend you kids for a regular feature on the news.

JAKE, NINA, and SEAN: We'll come *after* school if it's not! Thanks!

Think Critically

1. Would Nina's interests help her become a news reporter? Why or why not?

2. Did you like this play? Why or why not?

3. What will probably happen next time Nina is told "no" by someone?

4. How can you tell that Nina has good friends?

5. What was the author's purpose in writing this play?

 Math

Newspaper Fractions Look at the front page of a newspaper. Make a list of the articles and then estimate what fraction of the front page each story takes up. Write some conclusions you can draw from your findings.

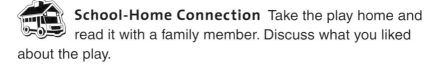 **School-Home Connection** Take the play home and read it with a family member. Discuss what you liked about the play.

Word Count: 1,105